Recovery *Workaholism*

Juanita & Dale Ryan

6 Studies for
Groups or Individuals

With Notes for Leaders

◤ *L I F E R E C O V E R Y G U I D E S*

INTERVARSITY PRESS
DOWNERS GROVE, ILLINOIS 60515

InterVarsity Press® is the book-publishing division of InterVarsity Christian Fellowship®, a student movement active on campus at hundreds of universities, colleges and schools of nursing in the United States of America, and a member movement of the International Fellowship of Evangelical Students. For information about local and regional activities, write Public Relations Dept., InterVarsity Christian Fellowship, 6400 Schroeder Rd., P.O. Box 7895, Madison, WI 53707-7895.

All Scripture quotations, unless otherwise indicated, are from the HOLY BIBLE, NEW INTERNATIONAL VERSION®. NIV®. Copyright ©1973, 1978, 1984 by International Bible Society. Used by permission of Zondervan Publishing House. All rights reserved.

Cover illustration: Tim Nyberg

ISBN 0-8308-1164-8

Printed in the United States of America ∞

14	13	12	11	10	9	8	7	6	5	4	3	2	1
04	03	02	01	00	99	98	97	96	95	94	93		

An Invitation to Recovery

Life Recovery Guides are rooted in four basic convictions.

First, we are in need of recovery. The word *recovery* implies that something has gone wrong. Things are not as they should be. We have sinned. We have been sinned against. We are entangled, stuck, bogged down, bound and broken. We need to be healed.

Second, recovery is a commitment to change. Because of this, recovery is a demanding process and often a lengthy one. There are no quick fixes in recovery. It means facing the truth about ourselves, even when that truth is painful. It means giving up our old destructive patterns and learning new life-giving patterns. Recovery means taking responsibility for our lives. It is not easy. It is sometimes painful. And it will take time.

Third, recovery is possible. No matter how hopeless it may seem, no matter how deeply we have been wounded by life or how often we have failed, recovery is possible. Our primary basis for hope in the process of recovery is that God is able to do things which we cannot do ourselves. Recovery is possible because God has committed himself to us.

Finally, these studies are rooted in the conviction that the Bible can be a significant resource for recovery. Many people who have lived through difficult life experiences have had bits of the Bible thrown at their pain as a quick fix or a simplistic solution. As a result, many people expect the Bible to be a barrier to recovery rather than a resource. These studies are based on the belief that the

Bible is not a book of quick fixes and simplistic solutions. It is, on the contrary, a practical and helpful resource for recovery. We were deeply moved personally by these biblical texts as we worked on this series. We are convinced that the God of the Bible can bring serenity to people whose lives have become unmanageable. If you are looking for resources to help you in your recovery, we invite you to study the Bible with an open mind and heart.

Getting the Most from Life Recovery Guides

Life Recovery Guides are designed to assist you to find out for yourself what the Bible has to say about different aspects of recovery. The texts you will study will be thought-provoking, challenging, inspiring and very personal. It will become obvious that these studies are not designed merely to convince you of the truthfulness of some idea. Rather, they are designed to allow biblical truths to renew your heart and mind.

We want to encourage realistic expectations of these discussion guides. First, they are not intended to be everything-the-Bible-says about any subject. They are not intended to be a systematic presentation of biblical theology.

Second, we want to emphasize that these guides are not intended to provide a recovery program or to be a substitute for professional counseling. If you are in a counseling relationship or are involved in a support group, we pray that these studies will enrich that resource. If you are not in a counseling relationship and your recovery involves long-term issues, we encourage you to consider seeking the assistance of a mental health professional.

What these guides are designed to do is to help you study a series of biblical texts which relate to the process of recovery. Our hope is that they will allow you to discover the Good News for people who are struggling to recover.

There are six studies in each Life Recovery Guide. This should provide you with maximum flexibility in how you use these guides.

Combining the guides in various ways will allow you to adapt them to your time schedule and to focus on the concerns most important to you or your group. All of the studies in this series use a workbook format. Space is provided for writing answers to each question. This is ideal for personal study and allows group members to prepare in advance for the discussion. The guides also contain leader's notes with suggestions on how to lead a group discussion. The notes provide additional background information on certain questions, give helpful tips on group dynamics and suggest ways to deal with problems that may arise during the discussion. These features enable someone with little or no experience to lead an effective discussion.

Suggestions for Individual Study
1. As you begin each study, pray that God would bring healing and recovery to you through his Word.
2. After spending time in personal reflection, read and reread the passage to be studied.
3. Write your answers in the spaces provided or in a personal journal. Writing can bring clarity and deeper understanding of yourself and of the Bible. For the same reason, we suggest that you write out your prayers at the end of each study.
4. Use the leader's notes at the back of the guide to gain additional insight and information.
5. Share what you are learning with someone you trust. Recovery is empowered by experiences of community.

Suggestions for Group Study
Even if you have already done these studies individually, we strongly encourage you to find some way to do them with a group of other people as well. Although each person's recovery is different, everyone's recovery is empowered by the mutual support and encouragement that can only be found in a one-on-one or a group setting.

Several reminders may be helpful for participants in a group study:
1. Realize that trust grows over time. If opening up in a group setting is risky, realize that you do not have to share more than what feels safe to you. However, taking risks is a necessary part of recovery. So, do participate in the discussion as much as you are able.
2. Be sensitive to the other members of the group. Listen attentively when they talk. You will learn from their insights. If you can, link what you say to the comments of others so the group stays on the topic. Also, be affirming whenever you can. This will encourage some of the more hesitant members of the group to participate.
3. Be careful not to dominate the discussion. We are sometimes so eager to share what we have learned that we do not leave opportunity for others to respond. By all means participate! But allow others to do so as well.
4. Expect God to teach you through the passage being discussed and through the other members of the group. Pray that you will have a profitable time together.
5. We recommend that groups follow a few basic guidelines, and that these guidelines be read at the beginning of each discussion session. The guidelines, which you may wish to adapt to your situation, are:

    a. Anything said in the group is considered confidential and will not be discussed outside the group unless specific permission is given to do so.

    b. We will provide time for each person present to talk if he or she feels comfortable doing so.

    c. We will talk about ourselves and our own situations, avoiding conversation about other people.

    d. We will listen attentively to each other.

    e. We will be very cautious about giving advice.

    f. We will pray for each other.

If you are the discussion leader, you will find additional suggestions and helpful ideas for each study in the leader's notes. These are found at the back of the guide.

Recovering from Workaholism

"My husband's not a workaholic, he just loves his work," my friend insisted as we sipped our ice tea and waited for our lunches to be served.

It was true. He did love his work. He spent most of his waking hours in work-related activities of one kind or another. And he had been rewarded highly for his efforts with promotions and the admiration and respect of his colleagues. It was also true, however, that his work life was slowly eating away at the foundations of his marriage. The same woman who insisted that her husband was not a work addict was so outraged at him that she was ready to pack her bags. Work addiction was putting their marriage at risk but, as with most addictions, neither of them could see the problem with clarity.

Work addiction is an addiction that has many things in common with other addictions. But it also has some important distinctives. Unlike addictions to chemicals or to food, which are viewed negatively in our society, addiction to work is usually socially rewarded. This is true not only in the workplace but, sadly, it is also true in the church. Work addiction, even if the work is ministry, is a problem. It is an addiction that is driven by the mood-altering effects of adrenaline which comes from the constant demands and pressures to perform. More fundamentally, work addiction comes out of a deep need to prove oneself good enough or valuable enough to be loved. This drive can be so powerful that people may fear for their survival if they are unable to work.

Wayne Oates defines a workaholic as "a person whose need for work has become so excessive that it creates noticeable disturbances in his health, happiness or relationships."[1] The ongoing consequences of work addiction are many. Work addicts live as if they are racing to their graves and have to accomplish as much as possible in the short time available. Work addicts also often complain of feeling out of control and believe that they are without a choice in matters related to work. They simply must "keep their nose to the grindstone" and keep pushing past the point of exhaustion. Work addicts are, therefore, lonely, depressed and lacking in self-awareness. For all their success, work addicts are desperately impoverished emotionally, spiritually and relationally.

It is important to remember that a person does not have to be successful in the business world to be a workaholic. He or she does not even need to be employed. It is possible to be a work addict in volunteer capacities at church or in the community. It is possible to be a workaholic housewife or mother. Whatever the arena for the work addiction, the needs of the workaholic are the same.

Recovery from work addiction involves more than abstinence from work. Work addicts will not be able to abstain from their drug of choice any more than a person who is addicted to food can abstain from food. But work addicts can practice sobriety, fasting from work on a daily and weekly basis. And work addicts can practice moments of resting, playing, reflecting and relating. It is possible to learn to say no to overcommitment; it is possible to acknowledge our limits, and it is possible to learn to ask for help.

God invites us to rest. God does not require us to prove ourselves to him through endless work. We do not need to strive harder and harder to gain God's approval. Quite the opposite is true. God offers us love and acceptance as gifts and invites us to a way of life in which the daily and weekly cycle is one of work and rest and play and relating. The studies in this Life Recovery Guide focus on these life-giving invitations from God.

May God give you the courage to respond to these invitations to grace and healing.

May your roots sink deeply into the soil of God's love.

Juanita and Dale Ryan

[1]Wayne Oates, *Confessions of a Workaholic,* p. 4.

1
An Invitation to Rest

"Slow down. You'll run faster." This was the advice which Coach Tom Tellez gave the six sprinters on the American Olympic team as they prepared for the 1992 competition. It is a paradox that applies not only to the art of sprinting, but also to the art of living.

Our Maker built into our bodies and souls a need for rest. We need to take regular breaks that allow us to step back far enough from our work so that we can regain perspective. These breaks may only take a few minutes. Or they may involve a half-hour to get some fresh air and to let go, for just that brief time, of whatever is our work. They may involve a quiet evening talking with our spouse or a close friend. Or a weekend away. Or a long vacation.

We function better, live richer lives (even work more effectively!) when we allow ourselves to rest on a regular basis. When we slow down, we run faster.

In spite of this, we resist taking care of ourselves in this basic way. God must have known how difficult rest would be for us. Perhaps that is why the Sabbath was important enough to be included in the Ten Commandments. God takes our need for rest seriously.

God invites you to rest. May you find the courage to struggle with this invitation until you can say a hearty, joyful yes to this life-giving invitation.

☐ **Personal Reflection** _____

1. What evidence do you see in your life that you might be affected by an addictive relationship with work?

2. What significant people in your life were/are workaholics?

3. What problems does your work create in your life?

☐ **Bible Study**_____

The apostles gathered around Jesus and reported to him all they had done and taught. Then, because so many people were coming and going that they did not even have a chance to eat, he said to them, "Come with me by yourselves to a quiet place and get some rest."

So they went away by themselves in a boat to a solitary place. But many who saw them leaving recognized them and ran on foot from all the towns and got there ahead of them. When Jesus landed and saw a large crowd, he had compassion on them, because they were like sheep without a shepherd. So he began teaching them many things. . . .

Jesus made his disciples get into the boat and go on ahead of him to Bethsaida, while he dismissed the crowd. After leaving them, he went up on a mountainside to pray. (Mark 6:30-34, 45-46)

---

1. What insights did you gain from your time of personal reflection?

2. This text is about Jesus and his disciples working and finding time for rest. What difficulties do they experience in finding time for rest?

3. How do the experiences of Jesus and his disciples compare with your own?

4. Jesus had sent his disciples out to heal and to teach. They had now returned and were reporting to Jesus about their experiences. Make a list of the things you feel God has called you to do.

What thoughts and feelings do you have about this list?

5. Because Jesus and his disciples were responding in helpful ways to the needs of the people, they were asked to do more and more. So much so that they had no time to eat. Describe a time when you were so busy doing good things that there was not enough time to do basic self-care such as eating or sleeping.

What is the potential danger of living this way on a regular basis?

6. Jesus offered his disciples an invitation in the midst of all the demands of their work. What are the components of this invitation?

7. How does this invitation to rest compare with what you would have expected Jesus to say in this situation?

8. How did Jesus model for his disciples creative flexibility in responding to the demands of work and the need for rest?

9. Imagine yourself in the middle of one of your busiest days or weeks. You are tired and hassled, but you feel a strong internal drive to keep pushing yourself. Now imagine Jesus coming to you and saying, "Come with me by yourself (or with one or two friends) to a quiet place and get some rest." What thoughts and feelings do you have in reaction to Jesus' invitation to you?

10. What could you do to accept God's invitation to rest? Include specifics such as (1) the quiet place you would choose; (2) whether you would go alone or with a friend(s) and which friend(s); (3) what would be restful for you; (4) the date or dates that you could go.

11. How might it help you to know that Jesus is the One who invites you to rest?

☐ **Prayer** _____

What would you like to say to God in response to the invitation to rest?

2

An Invitation
to Receive Help

"Thanks, but I can do it myself."

Many people who become addicted to work grew up having to do things for themselves. They did not receive the attention or help with skill-building that every child needs. So whatever they managed to learn, they learned on their own. Sometimes this independence can lead to appropriate resourcefulness. For many people, however, it leads to a kind of toxic self-reliance and rigid self-sufficiency that make it difficult to ask for or to receive help.

Many workaholics also experienced in childhood the kind of criticism that creates a need to work harder and harder to gain approval. Others may have received attention only for their achievements— a kind of affirmation that easily leads to a drive to work harder and harder to gain the attention every child needs.

As a result of these dynamics, workaholics believe they have to continuously function at a high level and that they must do so by themselves. Workaholics often do not think of asking for help. Not from their fellow workers. Not even from God.

In this text, another invitation to rest is offered. It is followed by an invitation to ask for help. We are invited to ask for help by a God who waits eagerly to respond to us with grace and compassion.

☐ Personal Reflection _____

1. Recall a time when you asked a friend for help. What happened?

2. Recall a time when you asked God for help. What happened?

☐ Bible Study_____

This is what the Sovereign LORD, the Holy One of Israel, says:

"In repentance and rest is your salvation,
in quietness and trust is your strength,
but you would have none of it.
You said, 'No, we will flee on horses.'
    Therefore you will flee!
You said, 'We will ride off on swift horses.'
    Therefore your pursuers will be swift!
A thousand will flee
    at the threat of one;
at the threat of five
    you will all flee away,
till you are left

> like a flagstaff on a mountaintop,
> like a banner on a hill."
>
> Yet the LORD longs to be gracious to you;
> he rises to show you compassion.
> For the LORD is a God of justice.
> Blessed are all who wait for him.
>
> O people of Zion, who live in Jerusalem, you will weep no more. How gracious he will be when you cry for help! As soon as he hears, he will answer you. (Isaiah 30:15-19)

---

1. What insights did you gain from your time of personal reflection?

2. What observations does this text make about the source of salvation and strength?

3. How do repentance, rest, quietness and trust lead to salvation and strength?

4. The text says that God offers us rest and quietness but we "will have none of it." How true is this in your life?

5. The people to whom this text was addressed were confident of their resourcefulness in the face of a military threat. Often, as workaholics, we also trust in our own efforts and competence to keep us safe. Restate in your own words what the text says about this approach to security.

6. We often work hard at religious endeavors out of a drive to please God, believing that the more we work, the more pleased God will be. How does this text challenge these thoughts?

7. The text makes a series of remarkable statements about God. List these statements.

Which of these statements is particularly meaningful to you? Explain.

8. What might change in your attitudes toward work if you were able to turn to God for help?

☐ **Prayer** _____

What help would you like to request from God?

3
An Invitation
to True Satisfaction

"I have worked and worked. I have achieved many of my goals. But I have not often been happy. Most of the time I have been lonely and exhausted. I often wondered what the point of it all was. Since being diagnosed with cancer, I have had time to reflect. I now realize that I would make very different choices in life if I had it to do over again. I would pursue my career—but not to the point of sacrificing my closest relationships. I think I may have missed the most important aspects of life, the things that really satisfy."

Work addiction robs us of the simple pleasures of life. If it is true that the best things in life are free, work addicts miss much of the best of life in their pursuit of money, status, success or recognition. We might miss our child's first birthday because we had to be away at an important meeting. Or we might miss the gift of sitting quietly, listening to the ocean. Or the joy of nurturing intimate relationships with good friends. Or the serenity of opening our hearts to God.

In the text for this study God challenges our desire to work hard at things that do not satisfy our deepest longing and invites us to experience the things in life that bring true satisfaction.

☐ **Personal Reflection** ————————————————————————

1. What do you believe gives life meaning?

2. If you were told that you had one year to live, what three things would be your highest priorities?

3. How significant of a change would this list of priorities be from the priorities implied by the choices you are now making?

☐ **Bible Study** ————————————————————————

"Come, all you who are thirsty,
  come to the waters;
and you who have no money,
  come, buy and eat!
Come, buy wine and milk
  without money and without cost.

Why spend money on what is not bread,
  and your labor on what does not satisfy?
Listen, listen to me, and eat what is good,
  and your soul will delight in the richest of fare.
  Give ear and come to me;
  hear me, that your soul may live.
I will make an everlasting covenant with you,
  my faithful love promised to David...."

Let the wicked forsake his way
  and the evil man his thoughts.
Let him turn to the LORD, and he will have mercy on him,
  and to our God, for he will freely pardon.

"For my thoughts are not your thoughts,
  neither are your ways my ways," declares the LORD.
"As the heavens are higher than the earth,
  so are my ways higher than your ways
  and my thoughts than your thoughts." (Isaiah 55:1-3, 7-9)

---

1. What insights did you gain from your time of personal reflection?

2. The text begins with an invitation to come, without money, to buy and eat. How would you restate this invitation in your own words?

3. The text then asks a difficult question, "Why spend money . . . and labor on what does not satisfy?" In what ways are you dissatisfied with the role of work in your life?

What do you think drives you to work hard when you experience limited satisfaction?

4. The text then makes a second invitation, this time with a promise: "Listen to me and eat what is good, and your soul will delight in the richest of fare." What would cause your soul to experience delight?

5. The language of the text grows even stronger as we are told to listen to these invitations so that our "souls may live." In what ways can a relationship with work rob your soul of life?

6. The text then reaffirms God's commitment to an "everlasting" relationship with us and, on the basis of that relationship, God invites us to change our thoughts and behaviors. What does the text say we need to change?

7. According to the text, what response can we expect from God if we change our compulsive thoughts and behaviors?

8. The text also reminds us that God's perspective is bigger than our own. What bigger perspective about life might God be wanting you to see?

How would seeing this bigger perspective help you to be less compulsive in relationship to work?

☐ **Prayer** ━━━━━━━━━━━━━━━━━━━━━━━━━━━━━━

What would you like to say to the God who offers to delight your soul?

4
An Invitation
to Humility

Susan: "But I have to do it. If I don't, it won't get done. Or it won't get done right, and I will have to come in later and clean up the mess."

Bob: "It really doesn't bother me if I skip meals and need to get by with only a few hours' sleep. What matters is that I get this work done. You just don't understand the pressure I'm under. I really don't have a choice. I don't like it either, but I am indispensable to this project."

Pastor Dan: "Normally I work about 70 hours a week. I am busy all the time. The ministry is so important, and there is so much need. I get calls every day from people needing my help."

Work addicts work without respect for human limits. Work can provide something we desperately long for—a sense of value, a feeling of worth. Because we do not believe we are valuable simply because we are one of God's lovable, valuable creatures, we are driven to find our value in what we do. "I am the only one who will do it right; I am indispensable; I can push way past my limits." This is the inner logic of human doings.

The biblical text invites us to experience ourselves in a very different way. It is the way of humility. Humility does not mean seeing ourselves as "bad" or "less than" or "worthless." An invitation to humility is an invitation to honestly acknowledge our limits, to learn to live within their confines, and to realize that our value comes from God.

☐ Personal Reflection ━━━━━━━━━━━━━━━━━━━━

1. What unrealistic ideas do you have about yourself that contribute to your overworking?

2. Which of your human limits and needs do you have a tendency to ignore?

3. What problems have you experienced physically, emotionally and relationally as a result of ignoring these limits?

☐ Bible Study ━━━━━━━━━━━━━━━━━━━━━━

Humble yourselves, therefore, under God's mighty hand, that he may lift you up in due time. Cast all your anxiety on him because he cares for you.

Be self-controlled and alert. Your enemy the devil prowls around like a roaring lion looking for someone to devour. Resist him, standing firm in the faith, because you know that your brothers throughout the world are undergoing the same kind of sufferings. (1 Peter 5:6-9)

---

1. What insights did you gain from your time of personal reflection?

2. The text begins "Humble yourselves under God's mighty hand." What benefits come from accepting this invitation?

3. What barriers make it difficult for you to humble yourself under God's mighty hand?

4. This text also invites us to cast all our anxiety on God. What anxieties would you expect to experience if you changed your compulsive attachment to work?

How would it help you to cast your anxieties on God?

5. The text states clearly that God cares for you. What thoughts and feelings do you have in response to this powerful statement?

How might seeing God as both mighty and personally caring help you to live with a greater sense of humility (that is, to live with respect for your limits and needs)?

6. The text invites us to be self-controlled and alert. We are invited

to take responsibility for our lives. What specific out-of-control behaviors do you need to take responsibility for?

What specific changes would you like to make so that you can live
within your limits?

7. The text also tells us to resist the devil. Other Scriptures call the
devil a deceiver and a condemner. In what ways do deceiving voices
or condemning voices contribute to your unhealthy relationship with
work?

8. In what specific ways do you need to resist these influences?

9. Spend a few minutes focusing on the image of God which this text gives us—a God who is powerful and caring. On a separate piece of paper list as many things as you can think of that make you anxious. Let the paper rest in your open palms. Present your list of anxieties to God. Ask God to care for you in all the ways you need to be cared for.

What thoughts and feelings do you have in response to this exercise?

☐ **Prayer** ————————————————————

What else would you like to say to the God who invites you to humble yourself under his mighty hand?

5
An Invitation
to Relationship

"We never have any time together, Joe. All you do is work."

"Don't start that again. We just went out on Friday night. How much time do you need? Don't you know that I work hard to give you and the kids a comfortable life?"

"I don't want all these things. At least not as much as I want to be with you. How come we can never talk about this? How come you can't hear me?"

"We already talked about this. You are always in my face about it. And believe me, I hear you. You are the one who isn't listening. I don't have any choice. I'm under a lot of pressure at work. Do you want me to get fired?"

And so it goes. Day after day. Addictions of any kind take on the position of the primary relationship in a person's life. When life is defined by tasks to accomplish and work to get done, relationships usually have a hard time competing for attention.

In the text for this study Jesus invites us to a different way of life. He invites us to a way of life characterized by love. He invites us to a way of life in which relationships are highly valued.

☐ **Personal Reflection** ─────────────────────

1. Think about the people in your life. List the people you consider to be your closest friends.

How much time have you spent with each of these people in the past month?

2. How has work affected your relationships with your spouse?

with your children?

with your friends?

with God?

☐ **Bible Study**_____

"As the Father has loved me, so have I loved you. Now remain in
my love. If you obey my commands, you will remain in my love, just
as I have obeyed my Father's commands and remain in his love. I
have told you this so that my joy may be in you and that your joy
may be complete. My command is this: Love each other as I have
loved you. Greater love has no one than this, that he lay down his life
for his friends. You are my friends if you do what I command. I no
longer call you servants, because a servant does not know his master's
business. Instead, I have called you friends, for everything that I
learned from my Father I have made known to you." (John 15:9-15)

_____

1. What insights did you gain from your time of personal reflection?

2. This text begins with a clear statement from Jesus: "I love you."
What thoughts and feelings do you have in response to these words
from Jesus?

3. The text suggests several ways in which Jesus expressed his love for his disciples. List as many ways as you can identify.

4. Jesus states that his desire is for us to experience joy and that joy is experienced in the context of loving relationships with God and with others. This emphasis on joy-full relationships may not be obvious to people who look for joy in work alone. What do you see as the relationship between love and joy?

5. How might it impact your compulsion to work if you were able to believe that God loved you and wanted you to experience joy?

6. Jesus gives this command: "Love each other as I have loved you." Describe specific ways you express your love to those closest to you.

7. What thoughts and feelings do you have in response to the fact that Jesus gives such a high priority to loving relationships?

8. How does Jesus' call to love impact you as you struggle to recover from workaholism?

☐ **Prayer** _____

What would you like to say to the God who loves you?

6
An Invitation to Celebrate

"All work and no play makes John a dull boy." So goes the old adage. But why is this? What is it about work that can make us "dull"? And what happens when we play or celebrate that is so life-giving for us?

An invitation to rest is an invitation to get away, to be quiet, to reflect. But an invitation to celebrate is an invitation to be active. To celebrate is to run, skip, jump, dance, laugh, throw a party. It is an invitation to restore our childlikeness, to abandon sophistication, to let go and enjoy.

Life is often difficult. Much of work is serious. Celebration takes us to the other end of the spectrum of human experience. It takes us to the places in life that are carefree and fun. We need these times and places for our physical, mental, emotional and spiritual health.

God understands our need for celebration. God is a God of celebration and joy. God does invite us to grieve with those who grieve, but it is equally true that God invites us to rejoice with those who rejoice.

☐ Personal Reflection _____

1. List ten activities you enjoy.

2. Next to each activity listed, indicate how often you have done that activity in the past month.

3. Make a simple plan to build one or more of these activities into your life this week or this month. Describe what you will do and when.

☐ Bible Study_____

Celebrate the Feast of Tabernacles for seven days after you have gathered the produce of your threshing floor and your winepress. Be joyful at your Feast—you, your sons and daughters, your menservants and maidservants, and the Levites, the aliens, the fatherless and the widows who live in your towns. For seven days celebrate the Feast to the LORD your God at the place the LORD will choose. For the LORD your God will bless you in all your harvest and in all the work of your hands, and your joy will be complete. (Deuteronomy 16:13-15)

"But the father said to his servants, 'Quick! Bring the best robe and put it on him. Put a ring on his finger and sandals on his feet. Bring the fattened calf and kill it. Let's have a feast and celebrate. For this son of mine was dead and is alive again; he was lost and is found.' So they began to celebrate." (Luke 15:22-24)

---

1. What insights did you gain from your time of personal reflection?

2. The Feast of Tabernacles was an annual celebration that involved the whole community. What reasons are given in the text for celebration?

3. What annual celebrations are particularly meaningful to you?

What would you like to do to increase the joy of annual celebrations?

4. The story of the prodigal son focuses on the celebration of an important event. What reasons are given in the text for celebration?

5. How can you celebrate important events?

What would you like to do to increase the joy of these kinds of celebrations?

6. What did the people in these texts do to celebrate?

7. What thoughts and feelings do you have in response to a God who invites you to celebrate?

8. What barriers might keep you from responding to this invitation?

9. What possible benefits do you see from building celebration into your life?

10. What specific kinds of celebrations would you like to plan to enjoy in the next two weeks?

☐ **Prayer** _____

What would you like to say to the God who invites you to celebrate?

Leader's Notes

You may be experiencing a variety of feelings as you anticipate leading a group using a Life Recovery Guide. You may feel inadequate for the task and afraid of what will happen. If this is the case, know you are in good company. Many of the kings, prophets and apostles in the Bible felt inadequate and afraid. Many other small group leaders share this experience of fear as well.

Your willingness to lead, however, is a gift to the other group members. It might help if you tell them about your feelings and ask them to pray for you. Keep in mind that the other group members share the responsibility for the group. And realize that it is God's work to bring insight, comfort, healing and recovery to group members. Your role is simply to provide guidance to the discussion. The suggestions listed below will help you to provide that guidance.

Using the Life Recovery Guides

This Life Recovery Guide is one in a series of guides. The series was designed to be a flexible tool that can be used in various combinations by individuals and groups—such as support groups, Bible studies and Sunday-school classes. All of the guides in this series are designed to be useful to anyone. Each guide has a specific focus, but all are written with a general audience in mind.

Many congregation-based recovery ministries use the Life Recovery Guides as part of the curriculum for "newcomers" groups. It can be a critical step in the recovery process to recognize that "recovery" is not a new set of ideas or the latest trend in popular psychology. Finding that the Bible is attentive to our struggles can often provide the courage needed to continue when the journey becomes painful.

We strongly recommend that careful attention be given to the group dynamics of the Bible study. Traditional Bible studies in the Christian community tend to be cognitively oriented, leadership tends to be well defined, commenting on statements by other participants is usually encouraged, giving advice is often valued, and sharing concerns expressed in the group with nonparticipants is often understood to be a kind of caring. Special attention will often be needed, therefore, to use the Life Recovery Guides in a way that teaches group participants the norms, values and group dynamics of the support group ministry to which the person is being introduced.

For example, if the Life Recovery Guides are used as an introductory experience that leads toward participation in a Twelve-Step group, then the group dynamics should probably resemble as much as possible those of a Twelve-Step group. Group facilitators should take time to carefully explain the purpose of the group and to introduce group participants to new group norms. It will probably take some time and practice, for example, to assimilate the concept of "cross talk." Groups using the Life Recovery Guides can help build a biblical foundation for what follows in the recovery process. But they can also help people to develop the skills needed to benefit from a support group experience.

Each guide contains six studies. If eight guides are used, they can provide a year-long curriculum series. Or if the guides are used in pairs, they can provide studies for a quarter (twelve weeks). The following are some ways that you might find it helpful to use the guides in combination with one another:

Topic	Number of Studies/Weeks	Guides to Use
Introduction to Recovery	12	Recovery from Distorted Images of God Recovery from Distorted Images of Self
Abuse	30	Recovery from Abuse Recovery from Shame Recovery from Distorted Images of Self Recovery from Fear Recovery from Spiritual Abuse
Addictions	30	Recovery from Addictions (Steps 1-3) Recovery from Guilt (Steps 4-9) Recovery: A Lifelong Journey (Steps 10-12) Recovery from Codependency Recovery from Workaholism
Family Dysfunctions	18	Recovery from Family Dysfunctions Recovery from Distorted Images of God Recovery from Distorted Images of Self
Divorce	30	Recovery from Depression Recovery from Loss Recovery from Shame Recovery from Broken Relationships Recovery from Bitterness
Grief and Loss	24	Recovery from Loss Recovery from Fear Recovery from Depression Recovery from Distorted Images of God

Preparing to Lead

1. Develop realistic expectations of yourself as a small group leader. Do not feel that you have to "have it all together." Rather, commit yourself to an ongoing discipline of honesty about your own needs. As you grow in honesty about your own needs, you will grow as well in your capacity for compassion, gentleness and patience with yourself and with others. As a leader, you can encourage an atmosphere of honesty by being honest about yourself.

2. Pray. Pray for yourself and your own recovery. Pray for the group members. Invite the Holy Spirit to be present as you prepare and as you meet.

3. Read the study several times.

4. Take your time to thoughtfully work through each question, writing out your answers.

5. After completing your personal study, read through the leader's notes for the study you are leading. These notes are designed to help you in several ways. First, they tell you the purpose the authors had in mind while writing the study. Take time to think through how the questions work together to accomplish that purpose. Second, the notes provide you with additional background information or comments on some of the questions. This information can be useful if people have difficulty understanding or answering a question. Third, the leader's notes can alert you to potential problems you may encounter during the study.

6. If you wish to remind yourself during the group discussion of anything mentioned in the leader's notes, make a note to yourself below that question in your study guide.

Leading the Study

1. Begin on time. You may want to open in prayer, or have a group member do so.

2. Be sure everyone has a study guide. Decide as a group if you want people to do the study on their own ahead of time. If your time together is limited, it will be helpful for people to prepare in advance.

3. At the beginning of your first time together, explain that these studies are meant to be discussions, not lectures. Encourage the members of the group to participate. However, do not put pressure on those who may be hesitant to speak during the first few sessions. Clearly state that people do not need to share anything they do not feel safe sharing. Remind people that it will take time to trust each other.

4. Read aloud the group guidelines listed in the front of the guide. These commitments are important in creating a safe place for people to talk and trust and feel.

5. The covers of the Life Recovery Guides are designed to incorporate both symbols of the past and hope for the future. During your first meeting, allow the group to describe what they see in the cover and respond to it.

6. Read aloud the introductory paragraphs at the beginning of the discussion for the day. This will orient the group to the passage being studied.

7. The personal reflection questions are designed to help group members focus on some aspect of their experience. Hopefully, they will help group members to be more aware of the frame of reference and life experience which they bring to the study. The personal reflection section can be done prior to the group meeting or as the first part of the meeting. If the group does not prepare in advance, approximately ten minutes will be needed for individuals to consider these questions.

The personal reflection questions are not designed to be used directly for group discussion. Rather, the first question in the Bible study section is intended to give group members an opportunity to reveal what they feel safe sharing from their time of personal reflection.

8. Read the passage aloud. You may choose to do this yourself, or prior to the study you might ask someone else to read.

9. As you begin to ask the questions in the guide, keep several things in mind. First, the questions are designed to be used just as they are written. If you wish, you may simply read them aloud to the group. Or you may prefer to express them in your own words. However, unnecessary rewording of the questions is not recommended.

Second, the questions are intended to guide the group toward understanding and applying the main idea of the study. You will find the purpose of each study described in the leader's notes. You should try to understand how the study questions and the biblical text work together to lead the group in that direction.

There may be times when it is appropriate to deviate from the study guide. For example, a question may have already been answered. If so, move on to the next question. Or someone may raise an important question not covered in the guide. Take time to discuss it! The important thing is to use discretion. There may be many routes you can travel to reach the goal of the study. But the easiest route is usually the one we have suggested.

10. Don't be afraid of silence. People need time to think about the question before formulating their answers.

11. Draw out a variety of responses from the group. Ask, "Who else has some thoughts about this?" or "How did some of the rest of you respond?" until several people have given answers to the question.

12. Acknowledge all contributions. Try to be affirming whenever possible. Never reject an answer. If it seems clearly wrong to you, ask, "Which part of the text led you to that conclusion?" or "What do the rest of you think?"

13. Realize that not every answer will be addressed to you, even though this will probably happen at first. As group members become more at ease, they will begin to interact more effectively with each other. This is a sign of a healthy discussion.

14. Don't be afraid of controversy. It can be very stimulating. Differences can enrich our lives. If you don't resolve an issue completely, don't be frustrated. Move on and keep it in mind for later. A subsequent study may resolve the problem. Or, the issue may not be resolved—not all questions have answers!

15. Stick to the passage under consideration. It should be the source for answering the questions. Discourage the group from unnecessary cross-referencing. Likewise, stick to the subject and avoid going off on tangents.

16. Periodically summarize what the group has said about the topic.

This helps to draw together the various ideas mentioned and gives continuity to the study. But be careful not to use summary statements as an opportunity to give a sermon!

17. During the discussion, feel free to share your own responses. Your honesty about your own recovery can set a tone for the group to feel safe in sharing. Be careful not to dominate the time, but do allow time for your own needs as a group member.

18. Each study ends with a time for prayer. There are several ways to handle this time in a group. The person who leads each study could lead the group in a prayer or you could allow time for group participation. Remember that some members of your group may feel uncomfortable about participating in public prayer. It might be helpful to discuss this with the group during your first meeting and to reach some agreement about how to proceed.

19. Realize that trust in a group grows over time. During the first couple meetings, people will be assessing how safe they will feel in the group. Do not be discouraged if people share only superficially at first. The level of trust will grow slowly but steadily.

Listening to Emotional Pain

Life Recovery Guides are designed to take seriously the pain and struggle that is part of life. People will experience a variety of emotions during these studies. Your role as group leader is not to act as a professional counselor. Instead it is to be a friend who listens to emotional pain. Listening is a gift you can give to hurting people. For many, it is not an easy gift to give. The following suggestions can help you listen more effectively to people in emotional pain.

1. Remember that you are not responsible to take the pain away. People in helping relationships often feel that they are being asked to make the other person feel better. This is usually related to the helper's own patterns of not being comfortable with painful feelings.

2. Not only are you not responsible to take the pain away, one of the things people need most is an opportunity to face and to experience the pain in their lives. They have usually spent years denying their pain and running from it. Healing can come when we are able to face our pain in the presence of someone who cares about us. Rather than trying to take the pain away, commit yourself to listening attentively as it is expressed.

3. Realize that some group members may not feel comfortable with expressions of sadness or anger. You may want to acknowledge that such emotions are uncomfortable, but remind the group that part of recovery is to learn to feel and to allow others to feel.

4. Be very cautious about giving answers and advice. Advice and answers may make you feel better or feel competent, but they may also minimize people's problems and their painful feelings. Simple solutions rarely work, and they can easily communicate "You should be better now" or "You shouldn't really be talking about this."

5. Be sure to communicate direct affirmation any time people talk about their painful emotions. It takes courage to talk about our pain because it creates anxiety for us. It is a great gift to be trusted by those who are struggling.

The following notes refer to the questions in the Bible study portion of each study:

Study 1. An Invitation to Rest. Mark 6:30-34, 45-46.

Purpose: To hear and respond to Jesus' invitation to rest.

Question 5. The potential dangers of the workaholic lifestyle are many. It takes a steady toll on our bodies to keep them pumped up with adrenaline, while we neglect our needs for food and sleep and times of quiet and play. It takes a toll on us emotionally. We grow fatigued and irritated and depressed. It takes a toll on us spiritually. We lose our perspective, coming to see ourselves as indispensable, wondering how God (and/or the company or ministry) would get along without all the work we produce. And it takes a toll on our relationships. The people closest to us begin to complain that they never see us. Or they may complain that when they do see us, we are preoccupied with work.

Question 6. The components of Jesus' invitation to rest are (1) to physically get away from the demands of life and work; (2) to find a quiet place to spend some time; (3) to go to this quiet place with a supportive friend or two and with Christ; (4) to rest—to have no agenda, no tasks to accomplish, no demands to respond to.

Question 7. Many people who are addicted to work may find this and the other invitations in these studies to be surprising, disorienting, confusing or unbelievable. People who are addicted to work often believe they are pleasing God. They are striving to be all God wants them to be. They may experience confusion or even anger when they hear invitations from God to a sober, serene lifestyle. Other people may find this invitation a welcome relief. It may provide the first permission they have experienced to stop working and to allow themselves to just be.

Question 9. The barriers to rest are many. Usually work addicts experience a "let down" feeling if they sit still too long. This is the feeling that comes as the body adapts to lower levels of adrenaline in the system. Addicts will also experience anxiety, worrying that they are not getting anything accomplished. There may also be the feeling of not being able to make the choice to rest. The statement "there is just too much to do, I can't rest now" is a serious statement for workaholics who feel they have no choice but to keep working.

It might help to be aware that "let down" feelings and anxiety will set in. Anticipate this experience, but also anticipate that these feelings will pass. When times of rest become a routine of life, these feelings will fade. And, with practice at resting, the sense of choice will increase. Experience will show that rest allows for more effective, energetic, creative work. Experience will show that no one is indispensable. The best medicine is to practice the discipline of resting until it feels good.

Study 2. An Invitation to Receive Help. Isaiah 30:15-19.

Purpose: To hear and to respond to God's invitation to receive help.

Question 3. Repentance refers to a change of heart and a change of behavior. Rest and quietness suggest a ceasing from work and a withdrawal from all the demands we face on a daily basis. Trust suggests placing our confidence in God to care for us. The combination of these activities renews our perspective. We cannot save ourselves or anyone else with all our hard work. We need saving. We need God. When we regain this most fundamental perspective, a quiet strength grows in us. Not a strength that comes from pushing ourselves past exhaustion but a strength that comes from remembering that we are loved by God.

Question 5. The historical situation was that Judah, under King Hezekiah's leadership, was experiencing a military threat from the Assyrians. Egypt was offering a partnership with Judah, and King Hezekiah was tempted to accept this offer.

The imagery used in this text suggests a desire to rely on our own power in the face of life's threats. God points out that we insist on running from his offers of rest and salvation. We will ride on horses and fight our own battles with our own strength. As a result, we will eventually find ourselves overwhelmed by the enemy. Our strength is not enough in life. We need God's help. Another choice would be to ask for God's help all along the way. King Hezekiah decided, with the prophet Isaiah's advice, to call on God for help rather than to join forces with Egypt. And God delivered them.

Question 6. God understands our need to rest and to trust in him. Our efforts are not what save us or strengthen us.

Question 7. The text makes several strong statements about God. God longs to be gracious to you. God rises to show you compassion. God is a God of justice. God will be gracious when you cry for help. God will answer as soon as you call.

Question 8. Turning to God for help restores our perspective. The act of "turning" is an acknowledgment that we are limited, that we cannot do it all alone, that we are not self-sufficient.

Study 3. An Invitation to True Satisfaction. Isaiah 55:1-3, 7-9.

Purpose: To hear and to respond to God's invitation to receive gifts, satisfaction and "soul delight."

Question 2. Water, wine and milk are being offered without charge to people who are thirsty. It is an invitation to have our deepest needs satisfied, not because we have worked hard and earned this nourishment, but because God offers this as a gift.

Question 5. Work addiction depletes a person physically, emotionally and spiritually. It robs us of the love and creativity and play that bring joy and satisfaction in life.

Question 6. The invitation of the text is to change destructive thoughts and behaviors. We are invited to turn to the Lord.

Question 7. People stuck in the addictive process are likely to experience invitations to change as shaming. "I invite you to change" will be heard as "you should change" or as "what is the matter with you? I can't believe you didn't change a long time ago!" Note carefully the character of God in this text. This is not a picture of an angry, abusive tyrant but a God who wishes to delight our souls, a God who is full of mercy and who freely pardons.

Study 4. An Invitation to Humility. 1 Peter 5:6-9.

Purpose: To hear and to respond to God's invitation to humility.

Question 2. Humbling ourselves under God's mighty hand requires that we remember and acknowledge that God is mighty; that we are his creatures; that we draw our life from him; that we are not independent, self-sufficient creatures; that we are fundamentally dependent on God. These perspectives help us to ask for the help we need and to live within our human limits. The benefits are that we might learn to live more sanely, feel less lonely, and be relieved of the burden of being superhuman.

Question 3. Some people may see God as harsh, punitive, critical.

God's hand may not seem gentle or loving. It may be difficult to trust God to care. People who have experienced abuse may take "humble yourselves" to mean "submit to abuse" or "grovel abjectly." Note, however, the proximity in this text of the image of God's hands "over" and "under" us. Being "under God's hand" leads to being "lifted up."

Question 4. The immediate anxieties will relate to concerns that the work will not get done and that terrible consequences will result. But the most basic anxieties that people will face are related to feelings that they have no value or meaning apart from their work—that they will lose their sense of identity and that they will not be accepted by God.

It is a wonderful experience to be cared for. Many people who work or minister compulsively experienced a deficit of care from their primary caregivers early in life. Letting God care for us can bring healing to this early, painful loss. Letting God take care of us in anxious times can comfort us, can give us peace and security and can bring us into a closer relationship of love and trust with God.

Question 6. Note the conjunction of "self-control" and "alert." "Control" focuses on behavior and "alert" focuses on attentiveness, but both qualities of character raise the same issue. Most of us know how to be either "overcontrolled" or "out-of-control." And most of us know how to be either "numb" or "hypervigilant" (super-alert). Sometimes we move back and forth between these extremes and experience very little of either appropriate self-control or appropriate alertness. Sobriety, however, requires both of these qualities. If we do not pay attention or if we pay attention compulsively, we will certainly set ourselves up for relapse. Similarly, either overcontrol or out-of-control leads back into dysfunction. There is much wisdom in the balance found in this text.

Question 7. Anticipate that some people will have difficulty with this reference to the "devil." Most people's thoughts and feelings about the devil are rooted in how the demonic is presented in popular media rather than in the biblical text. Try to avoid getting into theoretical discussions about evil. The point of this text is to alert the reader to danger. Our recovery takes place in a hostile environment. Recovering alcoholics will be exposed to thousands of advertisements for alcohol. And recovering work addicts will also be exposed to many situations which seem designed to encourage relapse. The focus of this question is on the effect of shame (condemnation) and distorted thinking (deception) on the process of recovery from work addiction.

Study 5. An Invitation to Relationship. John 15:9-15.

Purpose: To hear and to respond to Jesus' invitation to relationship.

Question 2. It is possible that some members of your group will focus on the conditional phrases of this text ("If you . . ."). People who have experienced affection, nurture and attention as conditional on their ability to perform will find it difficult to experience God's love as unconditional. If parental love and nurture were available to "good little boys and girls" but withheld from "disobedient children," then people will expect God to behave in similar ways. Notice that the phrase "if you obey my commands" is bracketed between two phrases about "remaining in God's love." It is not that our obedience creates God's love for us, rather it is God's love for us which is the certain foundation on which our understanding of obedience can be built. To see "obedience" as a condition for God's love is an example of "not remaining in God's love"—it is projecting our experience of dysfunctional and abusive relationships onto a loving and grace-full God.

Question 3. Jesus expressed his love for his disciples by (1) directly telling them that he loved them; (2) expressing his desire for their well-being and their joy; (3) being willing to lay down his life for them; (4) calling them friends; (5) telling them everything he learned from the Father.

Question 4. We were created to be in relationship with God and with others. We are relational beings. It is relationships of love that bring us true joy.

Question 5. Often, the "engine" of workaholism is the drive to be accepted and loved. We seek to prove ourselves to God and to others through our work. As we begin to experience God's love for us as a gift, our drive to earn this love will lessen.

Study 6. An Invitation to Celebrate. Deuteronomy 16:13-15; Luke 15:22-24.

Purpose: To hear and to respond to God's invitation to celebrate.

Question 2. In the passage from Deuteronomy, the people are instructed to party for a week to celebrate God's blessing on the work of their hands. This was an annual event and no doubt was a high point in the annual calendar.

Question 4. In the story of the prodigal son, Jesus uses the messianic feast theme to emphasize God's desire to "make merry." It is the triumph of grace over shame—the triumph of the values of God's kingdom—that leads to celebration.

Question 6. The celebrations in these texts are social events. Celebration is a community activity. Also, these events are accompanied by the cessation of work. Most work addicts will find it difficult to enjoy social celebrations and will need practical training in the how-tos of simple celebrations.

Question 8. The barriers to celebration are many. Work addicts may experience celebration as inefficient, as frivolous, as unnecessary, or as distracting from the mission or task. These forms of resistance to joy are often rooted in childhood trauma. If we learn early in life that joy is a fundamentally inappropriate experience, it will take some discipline and time to learn the skills of celebration as an adult.

For more information about Christian resources for people in recovery and subscription information for STEPS, the newsletter of the National Association for Christian Recovery, we invite you to write to:

The National Association for Christian Recovery
P.O. Box 11095
Whittier, California 90603

LIFE RECOVERY GUIDES FROM INTER-VARSITY PRESS
By Dale and Juanita Ryan

Recovery from Abuse. Does the nightmare of abuse ever end? After emotional, verbal and/or physical abuse how can you develop secure relationships? Recovery is difficult but possible. This guide will help you turn to God as you put the broken pieces of your life back together again. Six studies, 64 pages, 1158-3.

Recovery from Addictions. Addictions have always been part of the human predicament. Chemicals, food, people, sex, work, spending, gambling, religious practices and more can enslave us. This guide will help you find the wholeness and restoration that God offers to those who are struggling with addictions. Six studies, 64 pages, 1155-9.

Recovery from Bitterness. Sometimes forgiveness gets blocked, stuck, restrained and entangled. We find our hearts turning toward bitterness and revenge. Our inability to forgive can make us feel like spiritual failures. This guide will help us find the strength to change bitterness into forgiveness. Six studies, 64 pages, 1154-0.

Recovery from Broken Relationships. Divorce. Family conflict. Death. We may learn to fear closeness because we don't want to experience another separation from someone we love. God wants to heal us of the pain of lost relationships. These studies help us discover how to risk love again and build healthy relationships that will endure. Six studies, 64 pages, 1165-6.

Recovery from Codependency. The fear, anger and helplessness people feel when someone they love is addicted can lead to desperate attempts to take care of, or control, the loved one. Both the addicted person's behavior and the frenzied codependent behavior progress in a destructive downward spiral of denial and blame. This guide will help you to let go of over-responsibility and entrust the people you love to God. Six studies, 64 pages, 1156-7.

Recovery from Depression. From time to time we all experience feelings of hopelessness in response to difficult events in life—broken relationships, death, unemployment and so on. Sometimes we are not able to work through those feelings alone. And we need to be pointed toward the source of hope. This guide will show you the way. Six studies, 64 pages, 1161-3.

Recovery from Distorted Images of God. In a world of sin and hate it is difficult for us to understand who the God of love is. These distortions interfere with our ability to express our feelings to God and to trust him. This guide helps us to identify the distortions we have and to come to a new understanding of who God is. Six studies, 64 pages, 1152-4.

Recovery from Distorted Images of Self. God created us as people who are to be loved, valued and capable. But sometimes we don't *feel* that we are really cared for. We mentally replay negative feedback again and again. These studies will show you how to escape those negatives and be restored to a true vision of yourself as a person of immense worth. Six studies, 64 pages, 1162-1.

Recovery from Family Dysfunctions. Dysfunctional patterns of relating learned early in life affect all of our relationships. We trust God and others less than we wish. This guide offers healing from the pain of the past and acceptance into God's family. Six studies, 64 pages, 1151-6.

Recovery from Fear. Our fears revolve around certain basic issues—intimacy, risk, failure, loneliness, inadequacy and danger. But God offers us support, empowerment and courage to face fear in all areas of life. This guide will help us discover how God can enable us to face our fears. Six studies, 64 pages, 1160-5.

Recovery from Guilt. Guilt is a distress signal that warns us that something is wrong. If we do not pay attention, we will continue in destructive ways. This guide offers help in working through the pain of what we have done to ourselves and others. Using steps four through nine of the Twelve Steps in conjunction with Scripture, these studies offer hope and help to get beyond guilt to forgiveness. Six studies, 64 pages, 1163-X.

Recovery: A Lifelong Journey. Recovery requires a commitment to keep growing and changing through prayer and discipline. In this guide you'll see how the last three steps of the Twelve Steps provide a model for your lifelong journey of recovery. By following the disciplines of self-awareness, confession, seeking God and asking for guidance, you will find continued healing and growth. Six studies, 64 pages, 1166-4.

Recovery from Loss. Disappointment, unmet expectations, physical or emotional illness and death are all examples of losses that occur in our lives. Working through grief does not help us to forget what we have lost, but it does help us grow in understanding, compassion and courage in the midst of loss. This guide will show you how to receive the comfort God offers. Six studies, 64 pages, 1157-5.

Recovery from Shame. Shame is a social experience. Whatever its source, shame causes people to see themselves as unlovable, unworthy and irreparable. This guide will help you to reform your self-understanding in the light of God's unconditional acceptance. Six studies, 64 pages, 1153-2.

Recovery from Spiritual Abuse. Because of negative teaching we have received, many of us have learned that we have to earn our way with God. We have come to experience the Christian life as a burden—and a source of deep shame. Through these studies, we will discover that we can be healed of spiritual abuse and find freedom and grace in Christ. Six studies, 64 pages, 1159-1.

Recovery from Workaholism. Hard work results in promotions, raises and the respect of colleagues. More important, it fills the need we have to be needed. But overwork also eats away at marriage and family relationships, while making friendships outside the office nearly nonexistent. It can create health problems as well as spiritual struggles. This guide is designed to help you break free of workaholism and accept the rest that God offers. Six studies, 64 pages, 1164-8.